"Who Wrote This Thing Anyway??"

"An entertaining – yet practical guide – to who wrote the Bible and why it's reliable"

By Cecile Kaiser

Illustrated By Earl Musick

Copyright © 2013 by Cecile Kaiser (Author) Earl Musick (Illustrator)

Who Wrote This Thing Anyway??
by Cecile Kaiser (Author) Earl Musick (Illustrator)

Printed in the United States of America

ISBN 9781625098399

All rights reserved solely by the author. The author guarantees all contents are original and do not infringe upon the legal rights of any other person or work. No part of this book may be reproduced in any form without the permission of the author. The views expressed in this book are not necessarily those of the publisher.

Unless otherwise indicated, Bible quotations are taken from The New International Version® of the Holy Bible. Copyright © 1973, 1978, 1984 by the International Bible Society. Used by permission of Zondervan Publishing House. The "NIV" and "New International Version" trademarks are registered in the United States Patent and Trademark Office by International Bible Society.

www.xulonpress.com

WHO WROTE THIS THING ANYWAY??

"An entertaining – yet practical guide – to who wrote the Bible and why it's reliable"

By CECILE KAISER

Illustrated by EARL MUSICK

About Cecile Kaiser

. . .

Cecile is the owner of "Heav'n Fun Comedy." She is a comedienne, author, speaker, and illusionist, entertaining audiences from California to Australia. Her programs include a wide variety from dinners and fellowships to community outreaches, fundraisers, and full retreats.

She draws on her 30 years of ministry to not only entertain, but share God's love and His Word. Cecile lives in California with her husband, Bill. They have been married 38 years and have six children and nine grandchildren.

Cecile serves on the Board of the Christian Comedy Association, and has worked with Clean Comedians, Ambassador Speakers Bureau, and Single Source Speakers.

Cecile has also written the popular comedy devotional, "Bee Of Good Cheer."

For more information on her ministry, please go to her website: www.heavenfun.com

About Earl Musick

• • •

Earl is a professional cartoonist, humorous illustrator, comedian, and speaker. His cartoon work has appeared on the web, in movies, television, newspapers, magazines, books, greeting cards, calendars, T-shirts, posters, coloring books, and advertising. Earl has also worked as a ghostwriter for syndicated comic strips and panels. He has made countless television and radio appearances and has been featured in many newspaper and magazine articles.

As a freelance cartoonist, Earl's clients include: ABC TV, PBS (where he was a featured guest), First for Women

Magazine, Walt Disney Company, U. S. Postal Service, Christian Broadcasting Network, Chicken Soup for the Soul books, Federal Bureau of Investigations, Gibson greeting cards, Longaberger Baskets, Go.com, Ellery Queen Mystery Magazine, Ohio Country Journal, Medical Economics, plus many more.

As a stand-up comedian/speaker, Earl has entertained audiences for years with a powerful presentation that reaches groups of all ages, from preschool to retirement. He shares his humor and motivational skills with organizations, conventions, corporations, associations, churches, and schools. Earl lives in Ohio with his wife, Debbie, two sons, Matt and Mark and two dogs.

Website: www.earlmusick.com

Dedication

. . .

This book is dedicated to my husband, Bill, the love of my life.

Table of Contents

• • •

"Faith is Faith, Right?" 17
"Prove What?" 19
"So Who Wrote the Bible?" 27
"That's a Long, Long Time" 29
"Who Said What?" 33
"Who, What, When, Where?" 35
"Where the Heck Am I?" 37
"Hebrew, Greek and What?" 41
"Strange Places" 45
"Just the Facts, Ma'am" 49
"Can the Bible Pass the Test?" 51
"What Other Things are Significant in the Bible?" . . .55
"Canonization of the Bible – Who put it together?" . .61
"So What? – Why Should I Care?" 67
"Other Important Stuff" 69
"Verses You Can Rely On" 87

Introduction

. . .

Ever wonder where the Bible came from? What about those Bible-toten' people screaming, *"Well, it says so in the Bible!"* Why in the world do I care what the Bible says? For all I know, a bunch of guys were tired of bowling one Friday night, decided to order pizza and wrote the Bible. What makes it different from the Quar'an or Book of Mormon or any other religious book out there?

If you are asking any of those questions, you are already way ahead of me. I was a Christian many, many years before I realized I needed to know the answers to such questions.

When I accepted Jesus into my heart, I bought the "whole enchilada" - believed it *all immediately* and just figured it was all by faith. BUT. . . that's not what the Bible says. In 1st Peter 3:15, the Bible says, *". . . Always be prepared to give an answer to everyone who asks you to give the reason for the hope that you have."* God wants us to know what we believe and why we believe it – otherwise someone may just come along and jerk your faith out from under you because you don't have a strong foundation. Besides, some people need the "facts," and if we are to be witnesses for God, we need to know the facts. Is God afraid of that? Heck no! He says, "Bring it on!"

So I am. . . .

Since I am not that smart, *most* of the information here is taken from the video series (it may be available in DVD by now) by Josh McDowell entitled, "Don't Check Your Brains at the Door," (Word Publishing) which covers much more than I have included here. It is a wonderful series. I encourage anyone to seek it out for more complete information.

I have also included information from *"Case for Christ"* (Zondervan Publishing) by Lee Stroble and various other sources so noted. My intent here is not to make you think I know it all. It is to pull sources together and put them in one place for you. I have used their main topic information and recreated it in my own weird way of writing.

ONE

"Faith is Faith, Right?"[1]

First of all, understand there are two kinds of faith—"blind faith" and "intelligent faith." What's the difference? So glad you asked.

An example of "blind faith": Our youth group is on one of our mission trips to Mexico. We are hungry and drive by a local taco stand. Yea, it looks a little dirty... mangy dogs inside, we chase cats off the tables, go into the "baño" and the cook walks out without washing his hands... besides there's no soap in the restroom anyway... but hey, we figure (or have "blind" faith), the Mexican government regulates its restaurants – right? So we eat dinner. . . and proceed to throw up 3 days. . .

"Intelligent Faith" would be to call the mission camp director, a person that lives there, knows the community, and knows from experience where to eat and where not to eat. Based on those reliable "facts" you make an intelligent decision where to have dinner.

We are told to have "Intelligent Faith" based on the *facts*, not "blind faith" like a bunch of lemmings jumping off a cliff because the one in front of us does. . .

TWO

"Prove What?"[2]

There are actually two ways to prove something: **"scientifically"** and **"historically."**

To prove something *"scientifically"* you have to create and recreate the same *exact* scenario in a controlled environment and record the outcome. Doing the same thing over and over, under the same circumstances, and recording the outcome each time. If the outcome is continually the same, it is then proven "scientifically."

For example: Let's see, does Ex-Lax work? You write in your journal, "Took Ex-Lax at 8:00 p.m.; 8:00 a.m. ran to bathroom." Next night, "Took Ex-Lax at 8:00 p.m.; 8:00

a.m. ran to bathroom." Next night, "Took Ex-Lax at 8:00 p.m.; 8:00 a.m. . . . ." I think you get the picture (probably more than you want to picture), but *scientifically*, you have proven Ex-Lax works.

Can we prove "scientifically" that Jesus walked this earth? NO! *We can't even prove that YOU exist "scientifically."* In order to do that, you would have to crawl back in your mother's womb and be born again. Having given birth. . . . . . noooooooo!

This is when the *other* method is used to prove if something is true or not (because not everything can be proven by the scientific method). It is the *"historical"* method. That is the method used in our courts today. Reliable evidence and eyewitnesses are sought out and presented.

To prove that you exist we have your birth certificate, cute little baby pictures and videos of you, and testimony of your parents, family and friends. All of which proves "historically" that you existed. The same is true for George Washington, Abraham Lincoln, Elvis Presley, the Beetles.... and even Jesus Christ.

Actually, people don't dispute that Jesus Christ was a real person that walked this earth. He is written about in many *other* documents, *besides the Bible*. The "Talmud," the Jewish holy book, records some of Jesus' miracles, but attributes them to magic.

Josephus, a first-century Jewish historian (he was also a Jewish priest and Pharisee... and if you didn't know, the Jews, especially the Pharisees, did NOT like Jesus. Remember, Jesus claimed to be God – and that's why they crucified him!). Josephus wrote *"The Antiquities,"* which is about the history of the Jews from Creation until 93 A.D. He also wrote *Testimonium Flavianum."* Here is a quote from this book:

> *"About this time there lived Jesus, a wise man, if indeed one ought to call him a man. For he was one who wrought surprising feats and was a teacher of such people as accept the truth gladly. He won over many Jews and many of the Greeks. He was the Christ. When Pilate, upon hearing him accused by men of the highest standing among us, had condemned him to be crucified, those who had in the first place come to love him did not give up affection for him. On the third day he appeared to them restored to life, for the prophets of God has prophesied these and countless other marvelous things about him. And the tribe of Christians, so called after him, has still to this day not disappeared."*

There is some question if Josephus wrote the entire portion or if it was enhanced (read *Case for Christ* by Lee

Strobel for the entire writing), however, it does verify that Jesus was the martyred leader of the church in Jerusalem, he was a wise teacher and established a wide and lasting following, and he was crucified under Pilate at the insistence of the Jewish leaders."[3]

Another man that wrote of Christians was Tacitus, a Roman historian. He stated that in 115 A.D., Nero persecuted the Christians as scapegoats to divert suspicion away from himself for the great fire that devastated Rome in 64 A.D. He also describes how the Christians were hated and tortured for the beliefs.

There is another source, a Roman named, "Pliny the Younger" (he was the nephew of Pliny the Elder). In Book 10 of his writings he also tells of Christians being tortured, here are the exact words:

"I have asked them if they are Christians, and if they admit it, I repeat the question a second and a third time, with a warning of the punishment awaiting them. If they persist, I order them to be led away for execution; for, whatever the nature of their admission, I am convinced that their stubbornness and unshakable obstinacy ought not to go unpunished...

They also declare that the sum total of their guilt or error amounted to no more than this: they had met regularly before dawn on a fixed day to chant verses alternately amongst themselves in honor of Christ as if to a god, and also to bind themselves by oath, not for any criminal purpose, but to abstain from theft, robbery, and adultery..."[4]

(Yea, we really need to execute those "awful" people. They are a definite problem – taking an oath to keep themselves from criminal activities!)

Again, these are writing of antiquity (old, old, old books) written by *non-Christians*. This is *not* from the Bible.

If you paid attention in World history, I'm sure you've heard of Nero, the Roman Emperor. In 64 A.D., he attempted to kill all the people who professed faith in the newfound Christian religion. Nero took great pleasure in other people's pain and he was thrilled with the idea of wiping the Christians from the face of the Earth. He would dip Christians in hot wax as well as impaling them on poles and then lighting them on fire – saying to them, "Now you are the light of the world." He also had them killed at the Circus Maximus in Rome as entertainment for crowds (I have actually seen this place).

Nero executed many people, as well as some of the original disciples, including Peter and Paul, because they would not recount their story of seeing Jesus after his resurrection.

If we never had a Bible, we could still know the following about Jesus based on ancient writings that are in existence today:

- Jesus was a Jewish teacher
- Many people believed he did many healings and exorcisms
- Many people believed he was the Messiah
- He was rejected by the Jewish leaders
- He was crucified under the rule of Pontius Pilate
- And. . . . despite this shameful death, his followers, who believed he was still alive, spread the faith so there were thousands of them in Rome by 64 A.D.
- People from all walks of life, men, women, rich, poor, slave and free worshiped him as God[5]

So you see..

JESUS WAS A REAL PERSON AND HE WALKED THIS EARTH.

Jesus was crucified around 30 A.D. or 31 A.D. The first book of the New Testament was written around 49 A.D.,

---

[5] Stroble, Lee *"Case for Christ,"* Zondervan Publishing, page 87.

so many people who were alive during Jesus' ministry were obviously still alive and kicking. They saw Jesus' miracles, they heard him teach, they saw him crucified and saw him *after* he rose from the dead. (The authorities tried to say the disciples crept by the guards, somehow rolled the huge stone away – that was also sealed closed and at the bottom of an incline – broke into the tomb and stole his body… and the guards… who were under penalty of death if the body was taken…. didn't notice??)

The people of his time MUST have believed he was God… or why else would they have allowed themselves to be tortured for his name? I most certainly would not allow myself to be fed to lions, skinned alive, cut in half, crucified, and all the other awful things they did to Christians if I did not KNOW for a fact that Jesus was who he said he was – GOD! Would you…. especially if you knew you and a group of your friends stole the body and it was a hoax?

THREE

"So, Who Wrote the Bible?"

Back to the original point. Who wrote the Bible? Did God write God's Word? Why is it unique? Why is it worth reading?

To begin with, let me say, **the Bible IS in complete agreement with itself**. That is very important to understand. Sometimes it does appear to disagree with itself, however, if you question people who study the Bible - your pastor, youth pastor—people who have studied the customs and languages of biblical times, you'll find out that the Bible *is* in complete agreement with itself. . . throughout the entire Book!

Just one example:

"For everyone who has will be given more, and he will have an abundance. Whoever does not have, even what he has will be taken from him." Matthew 25:29 (NIV)

You're thinking. . . . "What about helping those in need?" Isn't that a contradiction? A Bible study will show you that Jesus is talking about faith, not money.

The Bible also addresses EVERY important area of life. No, not what you're gonna wear for that hot date Friday night. Even though some may consider it life or death, I'm talking every *important* issue like life, death, marriage (some men do see marriage and death as one in the same), relationships, raising children, abortion, homosexuality, purity, friendship, and the list goes on and on, but I'll stop now 'cause I want to finish this book before the turn of the century.

Why do I mention this? *That's what makes the Bible so amazing! The Bible never contradicts itself!*

Here Goes. . .

FOUR

"That's a Long, Long Time!"

*The Bible was written over a period of 1500 years!
That's over 40 generations.*[6]

Now, I don't know about you, but I didn't have a lot in common with my parents (surprise, surprise) and I had ABSOLUTELY NOTHING in common with my grandparents. They were weird!

I grew up in the 60's and 70's in the "hippie" generation. I was not raised in a Christian home and my idea of morals was extremely different from my parents and eons apart - like Earth to Pluto - from my grandparents. And that's only two generations. Imagine 40 generations!

How could people 40 generations apart even begin to think alike on *anything*, let alone the important issues in life?

In the 50's and 60's it was, "Hey Dad, just 'cause my boyfriend wears a leather jacket and rides a motorcycle, doesn't mean he's a bad guy." In the 70's and 80's it was, "Hey Dad, just 'cause my boyfriend has hair longer than I do and drives a VW bus that says, 'Make Love Not War', doesn't mean he's a bad guy." Now it's, "Hey Dad, just 'cause he has purple spiked hair, earrings, tattoos, and most of his face pierced, doesn't mean he's a bad guy."

Today, on Sunday afternoons, my husband, along with most of the other men on the planet, watch football, basketball, baseball, soccer, golf, fishing, bowling or whatever sport they can find. . . . and now, new technology allows them to watch 3 or 4 at a time! In the first century, people would gather in a stadium for entertainment, watching Christians being tortured or gladiators kill animals or each other (probably where reality TV is headed!).

It was only a few hundred years ago that people thought the world was flat and that you could sail off the end. They also believed the earth was the center of the solar system. No one knew about the unseen world of atoms and germs.

Heck, I grew up and survived without a dishwasher and our telephone had a party line - which meant we had to wait until the other neighbor was off the phone before we could use it! There were no microwaves, and personal computers were totally unheard of. . . . let alone cell phones, 3G, 4G, X-Box, or play stations. I remember "Get Smart" (a spy show) where the character had a "shoe phone" and we all thought that was far fetched!

I say it again, how could we possibly have anything in common with those people, especially on important issues of life?

If the Bible were not inspired by God - or as it says in the Bible, "all Scriptures are God-breathed," there is NO WAY on this earth it would agree with itself across 1500 years!

"All Scripture is God-breathed and is useful for teaching, rebuking, correcting and training in righteousness" (2 Tim 3:16)

FIVE

"Who Said What?"

The Bible was written by more than 40 different authors [7]
(In some books of the Bible, the author is not identified).

How more than 40 different people could agree on anything, let alone really important issues, is totally amazing. A committee or group of people can't ever agree on anything. I once spent three weeks on a committee just trying to agree on the table decorations! We'd still be sitting there if we were trying to agree on "life" issues. Everyone has their own opinion and wants to express it!

(I'm sure God made Adam first, 'cause if He had made Eve first she would have argued with Him on how to make

Adam.... "Lord, I think the biceps should be bigger...and understanding.... he should care more about MY feelings. And he should love to do more chores around the garden... and maybe he could bare the children... and have the hot flashes!*)*

SIX

"Who, What, When, Where?"

The Bible was written in all times of life: happiness, sadness, fear, joy, war and peace. It was also written in all geographical areas: from the mountains to the ocean, and from the valley to the mountaintop. It was written by people from all walks of life: kings to shepherds, rich to poor.[8]

Maybe that doesn't sound too important to you, but think about it; on one hand, you have a king who has more wealth than he could ever spend in a lifetime. Someone helps him dress in the finest clothes, prepares a banquet meal for him every night, and cleans up the castle for him. He doesn't do *anything* without someone tending to his needs.

On the other hand, you have a street guy who lives in a cardboard box and his banquet consists of a half eaten Big Mac he found in the garbage.

If you interviewed these two people on the important issues of life such as home, family, money, raising children, marriage. . . do you think they'd have the same opinion? Not likely! Yet, the Bible does. . . and they totally agree with each other - because it is God-inspired, not man's thoughts and opinions.

SEVEN

"Where the Heck Am I?"

How about being written in different geographical areas?[9]

We live in a tiny town in the mountains - Arnold, CA. I'll never forget the first time my children went to the city and found out the mailman actually went to homes and delivered mail (we *have* to go to the post office). They were amazed! Then we passed a corner where a bunch of people were gathered, my daughter asked, "Are those bums?" – *it was a bus stop*. My kids had never seen a bus stop, or a parking meter for that matter. Arnold has no traffic lights or traffic, no cabs, and only recently, a bus that covers the entire county. On their driving test they didn't even know what "light rail" was. We don't have gangs or crime like you see in the cities. If someone asked their opinion on "social" problems – they would have a much different answer than someone living in the city.

Another example: You've had an awful day. Your car broke down on the way to school. You were late to class and received detention. Pop quiz in geometry, and even though you knew the stuff, you failed. Your boyfriend or girlfriend, depending on who's reading this, broke up with you two days before the prom. It has *not* been a good day.

However, your best friend woke up to a surprise. Her parents had a new car sitting in the driveway with her name on it. She "aced" the geometry test and didn't even study. The hot guy in American Studies asked her out. . . and to top it off, when she got home her parents agreed to send her to Europe for the summer.

If I were to sit these two different individuals down that evening and ask them their opinion of life, imagine the differing views they would have.

That is exactly what happened with the Bible. It was written at "all" times of life, in "all" different places, under different circumstances, and by people from "all" walks of life, in peace, in war, in famine, in wealth, in fear and in safety... and yet, it completely agrees with itself. *And that is because the Bible was not man-written, but inspired by God. The Bible is God's words. The writer's thoughts and history were not part of the equation.*

Are you exhausted now... all this information jammed into your head at one time. Well, go get an energy drink, cause I'm not done yet. . . .

EIGHT

"Hebrew, Greek and What?"[10]

Next we are going to add to the mix the fact that the Bible was written in 3 different languages: Hebrew, Greek and Aramaic.

Have you ever taken a foreign language? If you have, you know we have words other countries don't, and they have words we don't have in English. In Greek they don't even use punctuation. That's why there are many different translations of the Bible. Biblical scholars keep trying to put the "original words" into our words and not lose the actual meaning. That's also why I said, sometimes the Bible seems to be in contrast, but you must understand the original Hebrew, Greek or Aramaic text to get the true meaning - 'cause it's usually not what we're thinking.

Thanks to Mark Lowry (a wonderful Christian comedian), here's an example: Ever notice how many sayings we use with the word "heart." "You broke my heart," "Put your heart into it," "I love you with all my heart," and probably a few more I can't think of right now. We use the word "heart" because to us it means the "center" of our feelings. Did you know, other countries use other organs? In fact, in the Old Testament of the Bible they used the "bowel" to describe the center of their emotions! Imagine what that would do to our love songs – "I left my bowel in San Francisco," or "I have the love of Jesus, love of Jesus, down in my bowel, down in my bowel." It would make Valentine's cards interesting though. Instead of exchanging chocolate candy, we could exchange Ex-Lax. (I know what you're thinking - is this woman obsessed with Ex-Lax or what?)

My daughter, Ashlee, and Luke, my son-in-law, taught English in Prague in the Czech Republic. It was at British school so they had to learn the Brit's form of English. She shared the following differences with me...

You can drink tea and have tea, because tea also means dinner. But then dinner means lunch. So, if a Brit is having tea, that's dinner. If they're having dinner, that's lunch.

And time is interesting. They'd say, I'll meet you at half 5. Now, does that mean 4:30 or half past 5, which would be 5:30? So if they want to meet you for dinner at half 5, you have no idea if they are wanting a late lunch at 4:30 or an early dinner at 5:30 - or is it a late lunch at 5:30?

Cookies are biscuits. I always thought they called them biscuits because it sounded healthier, but really, a cookie is a cookie.

Chips are fries. Crisps are chips. And tortilla chips are nachos (whether there is cheese or not).

If someone has lost the plot, it means they have no idea what's happening anymore.

If something is chalk a block it's just loaded up. As in, the pizza was chalk a block full of toppings.

Tennis shoes are trainers.

Running pants are tracksuit bottoms. Pants are trousers. Underwear are pants. You can actually say, "ah, pants," and have that be like "dang it."

They always laughed at how excited we American's were about simple little things. If we had a great night out, we'd say it was "fantastic," or even "magical." They'd unenthusiastically say, "It was lovely," "the food was nice." And the fact that we use exclamation points in our writing cracks them up. They can't understand our enthusiasm for everything.

Soccer is football. Our football is ridiculous, but, in their eyes, basically like rugby.

Driving more than 20 minutes to get somewhere is unheard of unless you're going on "holiday" for a week (they never say vacation).

Oh, and Santa is called Father Christmas.

And that is from a country that speaks the same language we do!

There's still more...

NINE

"Strange Places..."

The Bible was written on three different continents: Africa, Asia and Europe.[11]

In case you haven't noticed, some countries have very strange traditions. We actually eat what some countries worship (cows) - and we worship (our pets) what they eat!

In some parts of Africa, women put plates in their lips to make them huge and that's considered sexy. Or they put huge rings in their ears making them almost hang down to their shoulders. . . oh wait. . . I just saw a guy like that yesterday!

In some foreign cultures, they take 13 year old boys, put them in the jungle overnight and if they survive, they are considered men and are allowed to marry. – All the girls about now are saying - "Gross. . . . marry a 'junior higher'" – and all the boys are saying, "Sex at 13, yea!"

(Hate to tell you, girls. . . some men still act like 'junior highers' at 40!)

If you think that stuff is weird, try going to a wedding in Scotland, where the bride is saturated in tea, eggs, custard, tar, anything goopy and disgusting, and then paraded through all the local pubs.

Or in Kenya, when a baby is born, the newborn is passed around to all the other women in the birthing hut so they can spit in the baby's mouth.

How about. . . "Bouncing babies in India" - In Solapur, a yearly non-religious festival is held in which babies are thrown from a 15-meter tower. Thank heaven, they don't really bounce –people are waiting below with a sheet to catch the babies. As a mom. . . . I would die before throwing my baby off a tower – okay, maybe a few people. . . but not a baby!

I just witnessed some culture shock. When we were on vacation some women from Europe evidently sunbathe without a bathing suit top. Imagine my shock to walk out to the pool and see half naked women (imagine Bill's shock - okay, probably not shock...). As I sat there one afternoon, the lady in front of me was sunbathing, everything hanging out, as an elderly gentleman (with sunglasses) walked by, r-e-a-l-l-y s-l-o-w-l-y. . . . then walked back by – really slowly – and back by – really slowly – and back by – really slowly. . . you get the idea. . . He probably told his wife, "Hey honey, I'm going to get some exercise." He just didn't say it was gonna' be walking for two hours around the pool filled with half naked women.

All this to say, how could people from such different cultures, such different ways of life, agree on such important issues in life? Without God, it's not possible.

TEN

"Just the Facts, Ma'am"

Are you starting to get the picture? How amazing is this Book?

- It was written over a period of 1500 years, on 3 different continents
- In 3 different languages
- By more than 40 different people
- From all walks of life
- In all times of life

YET, IT TOTALLY AGREES WITH ITSELF ON ALL THE IMPORTANT ISSUES OF LIFE!

THERE IS NO OTHER BOOK IN HISTORY LIKE IT!!

ELEVEN

"Can the Bible Pass the Test?"[12]

Test, what test? Crud, I didn't study!

There are actually standards used by the "educational community" to determine the accuracy and reliability of books of antiquity (as I said, really old books). *Standards such as the number of surviving original manuscripts, circulation, and number of years between writings and the historical event.*

Original Manuscripts

The "educational community" makes you study books by people such as Pliny the Younger, Plato, Caesar, Tacitus, Aristotle, Sophocles, and Homer. All of these have been determined by the "educational community" to be of historical value and worth studying.

Here are the number of *surviving original manuscripts* that have been found (as of 1985):

> Pliny the Younger (History) – 7
> Plato (Tetralogies) – 7
> Caesar (Gallic Wars) – 10
> Tacitus (Annals) – 20
> Aristotle – 49
> Sophocles – 193
> Homer (Iliad) – 643

Want to know how many original portions of manuscripts of the New Testament have been found - and this is as of 1985 - that's more than 25 years ago... 24,633!! Let me say that again – 24,633!!

Based on the guidelines of the "educational community" and what they determine to be reliable and accurate, they should *automatically* consider the Bible - because it far exceeds anything they have!

What about circulation?

The Bible far exceeds any of the "books of antiquity." Again, these statistics were from1985. **The Bible is #1 in circulation in all of history.** Bible Societies alone have printed over 2,582,000 Bibles and portions of scripture since 1800 (when the printing press was invented).

In order to print that many Bibles and portions of scripture you'd have to print one copy every 3 seconds / 22 every minute / 1200 per hour / 32,856 per day / 12,000,000 every year since 1800.

If you laid that much scripture end to end, it would be enough to go around the entire earth over 1,000 times.

It's true, this in itself does not verify that this is the Word of God, but by the "educational community's" own standards, they should at least, consider the validity of the Bible.

Time between the writing and actual events?

Many of the famous writings were written *centuries* after the event, leaving room for "exaggeration and embellishing" to be included. However, the New Testament is based on eyewitness accounts and letters from the actual writers.

Matthew (the tax collector) and John were Jesus' disciples. Mark walked with Peter and Luke walked with Paul. The first writings appeared within about 16 years of

Jesus' death and resurrection, Galatians and James in 49 A.D. *Most of the population that was alive when Jesus walked this earth. . . was still alive!* If the writings were false, the people would have known it!

It is now eleven years, since the World Trade Center bombings in New York on September 11, 2001. You were alive when it occurred. In fact, everyone can probably tell you what they were doing when they heard about it. (The same is true for those of us who were alive when President Kennedy was assassinated. I was in math class. I can still picture the class today.) Point being, you can say with certainty that it *did* happen. The same is true for those alive when Jesus walked this earth and the more than *500* people who saw him after he was crucified – dead – and then alive again!

The "educational community" gladly accepts writings as authentic that were written *hundreds of years* after the event – they certainly should consider the Bible as accurate as the *entire* New Testament was written within about 62 years of the time Jesus walked the earth.

TWELVE

"What Other Things are Significant in the Bible?"

How about Bible prophecy? [13]

God used prophets to relay His messages to the people. If they were false prophets... their life span was very short. They had to be correct 100% of the time. If they were wrong – even once – they were killed!

> "But a prophet who presumes to speak in my name anything I have not commanded, or a prophet who

speaks in the name of other gods, is to be put to death." Deuteronomy 18:20

There are approximately 2500 prophecies in the Bible. Of those, approximately 2000 have come true – *exactly as predicted!* (The other 500 are still to come.)

These predictions were made *hundreds of years* before they happened. Now as you just learned, if you actually read the preceding, *many of the books of the Bible were written by different people in different countries over a 1500 year period* – yet their prophecies came true – exactly as predicted. By the way, the chances of that happening is pretty much impossible. . . less than one in 10^{2000} (that's 1 with 2000 zeros after it!). I've also heard it described like this: If you took one silver dollar – marked it – and dropped the silver dollar somewhere onto the State of Texas which was covered with a foot (deep) of silver dollars. Then you reached down and randomly picked out that *one* particular marked silver dollar! (Sorry, I don't remember where I read it.) I think you get the point. The chances of the prophecies being that accurate – if they were not directed by God – would be impossible!

Here are a few:

- Recorded in Micah 5:2. The prophet Micah, around 700 B.C., (Jesus was born around 4 B.C.) predicted the tiny village of Bethlehem would be the birthplace of Israel's Messiah, Jesus. Fulfillment of this prophecy is one of the most widely known and widely celebrated facts in history.

- Recorded in Zechariah 11:12-13. The prophet Zechariah, in the fifth century B.C., predicted that the Messiah would be betrayed for thirty pieces of silver, and that money would be used to buy a burial ground for Jerusalem's poor foreigners. That is *exactly* what happened hundreds of years later. Judas Iscariot betrayed Jesus for the exact sum of thirty pieces of silver. After Judas committed suicide, that money went to buy a "potter's" field to bury the poor foreigners! It is recorded in Matthew 27:3-10, hundreds of years later!

- Recorded in Zechariah 12:10, and again in Psalms 22, both King David and Zechariah describe the Messiah's death as crucifixion... **but the Romans did not invent crucifixion until 400 years after this prophecy!** Zechariah talks about him being "pierced" while David predicts "all his bones will be out of joint" - which is what happens when you're hung on a cross for hours, sometimes days on end. Further, David says "none of his bones will be broken."

This all came about hundreds of years later when Jesus died on a Roman cross. As I said, it could take days to die on a cross, but since it was the eve of the Sabbath, they wanted Jesus' death over so they could take his body down before sundown. (Jewish culture would not allow people to do any kind of work during the Sabbath. Taking someone off the cross would have been considered work - even though killing an innocent person didn't seem to be a problem!)

Normally, if the Romans wanted to speed up the crucifixion they would break the person's legs which would cause them to suffocate quickly. In Jesus' case, he had already given up his life so they *did not* break his legs. Also, they "pierced" his side with a spear and blood and water flowed out, showing he was already dead.

There is a scientific reason why "blood and water" flowing showed Jesus was already dead. As I said, the crucified person died from suffocation when he could no longer push up on his legs to grab a breath -(breaking someone's legs would obviously keep them from being able to push up). On the other hand, if someone dies of heart failure, water collects in the pericardium sac around the heart. Jesus, had already given his life so when the guard rammed the spear into Jesus' side and up into the sac around the heart – the "water" that flowed showed Jesus died of heart failure - or a broken heart).[14]

Both of those predictions were accurate.

- Even more poignant is the prophecy of Isaiah, written around 681 B.C. as seen in Isaiah 53:5-9. Isaiah says, "He (the Messiah) will be pierced for our transgressions and crushed for our iniquities, and by his wounds we are healed." Further it says that "all our sin will be put on him" – he will be "led like a lamb to slaughter" and "he will not open his mouth" – and, "he had done nothing wrong." That is *exactly* what Jesus did. He was falsely accused, falsely arrested, put through a mock trial, and did not answer back when questioned. Jesus hung on the cross and died for our sins, so we could be made right in God's eyes.

How in the world could Isaiah know this more than 600 years before the event? How could he even know about Jesus? Only one way - the writings of the Bible are God inspired.

And. . . *there are hundreds more*. Please check the website I have listed in the endnote if you'd like to read more.[15]

All the time, people are reading Nostradamus or their horoscope. . . . or consulting psychics, even believing fortune cookies, but they doubt the Bible??

THIRTEEN

"Canonization of the Bible – Who Put This Thing Together?"

How did we come out with the 66 books in the Bible? Canonization of the Bible means - how the 66 books in the Bible were chosen.

In studying this issue, I found it *very* hard to put it into a few words and write it in a way you'd enjoy reading it! (And I may not have accomplished that!) But, I feel it's more important to give you information on how the books were chosen as opposed to all the different church councils' involvement. In the endnotes I have listed two great websites, and "The New Evidence That Demands a Verdict," by Josh McDowell that can fill in the information, if you'd like more.

As I said at the start, a bunch of guys didn't just sit around one Friday night and decide to write the Bible. But who actually chose the books that are included in our Bible today? ***The truth is. . . . God chose the books He wanted in there. . . men just had to decipher God's will.***

I'd also like to note that the Old Testament (the Hebrew Bible) is substantially the same as the original writings, with vowels added and a few other additions to make it easier to read.[16]

I'm sure you've heard of the Dead Sea Scrolls. When they were discovered in 1947, they gave us a Hebrew text from the second to first century B.C. of all but one of the books (Esther) of the Old Testament. This was an incredible discovery, for it provided a much earlier check on the accuracy of the Old Testament text, which has now proved to be extremely accurate. Please go to the website listed to understand the unbelievable care that was taken to ensure that each Old Testament copy handwritten (no copy machines. . . no cut and paste) by scribes was perfect. [17]

There were guidelines the church leaders (several different councils of church leaders over the early centuries) used to decide which books were God's inspired word and not man's.

That criteria was as follows:

1. Was the book written by a prophet of God?
2. Was the writer confirmed by acts of God?
3. Did the message tell the truth of about God?
4. Does it come with the power of God?
5. Was it accepted by the people of God?[18]
6. Was the author an apostle or have a close connection with an apostle?
7. Did the book contain consistency of doctrine and orthodox teaching?
8. Did the book bear evidence of high moral and spiritual values that would reflect a work of the Holy Spirit?[19] (So the crazy people that say, "God told me to kill so-and-so," they're listening to the wrong voice. . . because God NEVER tells you to do anything against His Word. - Just thought you needed to hear that tidbit!)

In looking to see if the books were accepted by the "people of God" in the early church:

- There are some 250 references in the New Testament to the Old Testament.

- In the New Testament itself Paul called Luke's writings to be as authoritative as the Old Testament for in 1 Timothy 5:18 Paul is quoting both Luke's (Luke 10:7) writing and Deuteronomy (25:4).
- Peter recognizes Paul's writings in 2 Peter 3:15-16.
- Some of the books of the New Testament were being circulated among the churches (See Colossians 4:16; 1 Thessalonians 5:27).

Church fathers (leaders in the early church), in their letters to one another, quoted the New Testament Scriptures more than 86,000 times. Their quotations have allowed scholars to reconstruct 99.86 per cent of the New Testament. There are only 11 verses in the New Testament that the church fathers apparently never cited.[20]

And from famous writers and historians with weird names from. . . well history:

- Clement of Rome mentioned at least eight New Testament books (95 A.D.).
- Ignatius of Antioch acknowledged about seven books (115 A.D.).
- Polycarp, a disciple of John the apostle, acknowledged 15 books (108 A.D.).
- Irenaeus mentioned 21 books (185 A.D.).
- Hippolytus recognized 22 books (170-235 A.D.).[21]

(Thank heaven I wasn't born back then. . . . I can't imagine what my mother would have named me. . . Cecile Athaline's bad enough!)

Additionally, the Bible has been proven to be historically reliable by many archaeological discoveries. To date, more than 25,000 archaeological discoveries have verified the names of persons, places, events, and customs mentioned in the bible[22]

Again, it is *vital* to remember that the church (or man) did *not* determine the canon. No early church council decided on the canon. *It was God, and God alone, who determined which books belonged in the Bible*. The human process of collecting the books of the Bible was flawed, (because we're . . . . human), but God, in His sovereignty, and despite our ignorance and stubbornness, brought the early church to the recognition of the books He had inspired.[23]

FOURTEEN

"So What? - Why Should I Care?"

Y ou have just learned why the Bible is so unique. *Of ALL the books written in history, there is more proof for the authenticity of the Bible than any other book ever written.*

If that is so. . . . then it is important to know what it says – and take it seriously!

The Bible. . . Old Testament and New Testament. . . all talk about the sin in man and the fact that God in human form, Jesus, was coming, and later came to earth to die for our sins so we might have an eternal relationship with Him. You see, the truth is. . . . all of us are going to live eternally! You choose. . . . smoking or non-smoking!

I say that jokingly, but the reality is not funny. Jesus actually warns us more about hell than He ever talks of heaven. He also says in the Bible – that we now know is true – that His desire is that *none* should perish. That's you and me.

The Lord is not slow in keeping his promise, as some understand slowness. Instead he is patient with you, not wanting anyone to perish, but everyone to come to repentance. (2 Pet 3:9)

FIFTEEN

"Other Important Stuff"

- **How special is our universe?**[24]

To believe that our universe evolved or just happened takes *far* more faith than believing a Creator created it.

I know what you're thinking. . . . "But they taught us in school we crawled out of a slime pit." (Be sure to watch for my next book, "I Know Some People Act Like They Crawled Out of a Slime Pit, But Did They Really?")

Here's my Atheist Pledge of Allegiance:

*I pledge allegiance to the flag of the United States of America, and to the republic for which it stands – one nation – under **NO ONE**, because **absolutely nothing** exploded forming our perfect universe – then it rained and rained on the rocks for billions and billions of years making a primordial sludge – that the first living thing crawled out of – managed to find a mate – then proceeded to evolve into every creature, animal and human alive today – against ALL laws of science and nature – but we refuse to believe there is a God – indivisible with liberty, justice and if you agree with us – freedom of speech for all.*

That's what they're teaching our children!!! Does that make sense? Scientists *cannot* make evolution work - so they keep stretching out the "time" in which it supposedly happened. Because if they admit there is a God. . . then everyone is accountable for their actions!

- Among all the other planets in space, Earth is the only one capable of sustaining human life. Look at the temperature – if it were any hotter – it would not sustain life. If it were colder – it would not sustain life.

- How about the oceans and the tides which are caused by the gravitational pull of the moon. If our moon were larger, we'd have huge tidal waves wiping out a large portions of our land. If our moon was smaller, we'd have no gravity and the oceans would be stagnant and die.
- Consider tap water - turn on the faucet and out it comes, right? Well, the solid state of most substances is heavier than the liquid state – but it is the exact opposite for water and ice. . . otherwise ice would sink instead of float. If water was like every other liquid, it would freeze from the bottom up instead of the top down – killing all ocean life, destroying our oxygen supply and make our earth uninhabitable.
- Let's take a look at some of the incredible creatures God created:
- Check out the Emperor Penguins. These birds live in the freezing cold of the Antarctic. They have a feather coat and a layer of blubber so they can withstand the freezing temperatures. But the most amazing thing about these animals is their care for their babies. In March, the adults come ashore (after spending the summer at sea eating and putting on weight – sounds like me), walking as far as ninety miles across the ice to the breeding grounds. When

they have found a mate (Matchpengiun.com??), they stay there until the female lays her egg... a very large egg, I might add. She lays the egg on the ice because there is no nesting material around... no nice soft straw or memory foam mattress... only ice and snow.

Now the problem... the mom and dad have to keep the egg off the ice because it will freeze like an "eggsicle" if it spends even a few minutes on it. The penguins have large feet and a flap of feathered skin down by their feet. The egg sits on the mom's feet, under the feathered skin, then she passes it to dad. Here's the sticky part! The mom will then walk back, ninety miles, to the water (I know some people who won't walk a half a mile to the store!) to gorge herself on food for about two months. All that time the male stands there.... holding the egg on his feet... not eating anything himself, as he cannot leave the egg on the ice to go look for food. As the egg is about to hatch, the female returns... *just in time*.... before the baby arrives and the male dies of starvation!

Also amazing is the fact that she can even find her mate among thousands of other penguins that look exactly alike. If it had taken her extra days to find her mate... or if she stopped to chat with a friend... or if she stayed out to sea one extra day, both the male and the baby would die.

Next it's dad's turn to go hit the buffet. He takes off for two months, eating as much fish as "penguinly" possible. He then does the same thing. He walks back, ninety miles, manages to find her and the baby amongst thousands of look-a-likes, just in time. (No dead-beat dads here.) One day later, or if he had stopped to shoot "hoops" with some penguin buddies, both mom and baby would have died of starvation.

If evolution and the "survival of the fittest" is true – these animals would have never survived. There is no room for error or miscalculation of when the penguins return from feedings, or if they let the egg sit on the ice even for a few seconds – they would die! There was no "practice makes perfect" in this case.

- There's another extraordinary bird in Australia called the Malleefowl. It digs a pit and fills it with decaying leaves and then piles sand on top. The female then digs a tunnel and lays her eggs. The eggs are kept warm by the heat from the decaying leaves. The bird then checks the temperature of the nest continuously, to make sure it is not too hot or too cold. Several times a day, she pokes her beak into the sand. Her tongue is so accurate, she can tell a change in temperature as little as one-tenth of a degree! If the nest is too cool, she adds sand. If it is too hot, she scrapes sand away. After some time, the birds hatch and dig their way to the surface.

Even if. . . and that's a big "if," natural selection or mutation could account for the bird's tongue, how could chance mutation "teach" the bird to use it's tongue in such a way or to build her nest in decaying leaves?

- Or how about the woodpecker. I know what you're thinking. . . common bird everywhere, even somewhat of an irritant. But it is an incredible example of how God created animals for a distinct purpose. They didn't just happen by evolution.

The woodpecker's feet are different than other birds. Other birds have to perch on a tree limb, but the woodpecker's feet have two toes pointing backward and two pointing forward allowing him to hang onto the side of a tree. In addition to that, their tail feathers are short and stiff, unlike other birds, so they can lean against them on the side of the tree while they beat their heads against the tree. Well, not exactly their heads, but their beaks. Also unusual about the woodpecker is the fact they have a spongy tissue behind their beaks acting as a "shock absorber" to be able to withstand the constant pounding on the tree, sometimes five to six hours a day! In all other birds the beak and skull are fused together in one piece.

"Other Important Stuff"

The woodpecker bores into the tree for a reason – for food. That brings us to the next amazing thing about this little bird, its tongue. The bird sticks its tongue down the hole he has bored and reaches one of the tunnels made by the insect. Its tongue then follows the tunnel until it finds the insect and then draws the bug out for dinner. Other birds have a tiny little tongue attached to their mouths, but the woodpecker has an amazing tongue. It is generally longer than the entire bird, and it curls around inside the woodpecker's skull and is attached to its head. Without that long tongue, the woodpecker could not retrieve its food and would die.[25]

If this bird evolved, how many, first of all, fell off the trees and died because their feet weren't able to hold them to the tree? How many killed themselves knocking their heads against the trees because the shock absorber hadn't fully developed? How many died because their tongue hadn't grown long enough to reach their food? It's absurd to think this little bird evolved. It would have been extinct before it even got started!

These are *only three* miraculous examples of hundreds upon hundreds in the animal kingdom, blowing away the idea of evolution and the thought that everything just "happened" by chance.

The truth is – our Earth is the only planet perfect for human life and, it was perfectly formed. God also created the wonderful creatures here on Earth. They didn't evolve or happen by chance!

- **"How can a good God send people to hell?" (Warning: this is a graphic description!)**

Let's be real here. What else could He have done for you? He left His throne in heaven and came to this world as a baby. His mother was not a queen, but the lowly peasant girl, which in the Jewish world, was considered barely above an animal. Jesus chose to walk this Earth knowing that the people *He created* would eventually crucify Him *on the tree He created!*

Speaking of crucifixion.... the Romans were pros when it came to torturing people. Talk about cruel and unusual punishment! If you were crucified, spikes would be driven into your wrists and feet, and as you hung on a cross, you would be dangling by your wrists and feet that had the spikes through them. Your arms would be pulled out of their sockets forcing you down, compressing your lungs making it hard to breathe. In order to actually breathe, you would have to push up on your feet (that would be your painful feet with the spike in them) to gasp for air.

This torture would go on for hours and hours, and possibly days, until you finally died.

On top of the crucifixion, Jesus was also beaten to within an inch of his life! Again, the Romans were masters at beating people. The whips were made of strands of leather and tied to the ends were bits of metal, broken pottery. . . anything sharp they could find. They would bring the lash down on the bare back – which hurt enough by itself – but when they pulled the lash back, it pulled out parts of skin with it. . . ripping the body wide open.

This is God!!! He *willingly* did this for us. He didn't have to. A harsh, unloving god would have left us on our own! Jesus came from heaven to walk among us, personally show us His love and kindness, knowing we were going to torture Him to death! ALL HE ASKS IS THAT WE BELIEVE IN HIM. . . FREE OF CHARGE! Again I say, what else could He do to make it any easier? It costs you nothing. . . *The cost to Him was enormous!*

- **"Why does a good God allow so much pain in this world?"**

If you're asking that question, you are certainly not alone! First, you have to realize there are 3 roads of thought:[26]

(1) Pantheism - which denies the existence of good and evil - because god is all and all is god. It's weird to me too.

(2) Philosophical Naturalism - which is evolution - and everything is a function of random chances and therefore, there is no good and evil - even weirder! I guess we shouldn't prosecute anyone for crimes because they evolved that way so they're not at fault?

(3) Theism, specifically Christian Theism. God gave us free will. If He hadn't, we'd be robots walking around or puppets on His string. What does love mean if you force it on someone? But. . . . by giving us free will. . . the choice for man was to do good or evil. Unfortunately, a lot have chosen evil.

The good news is God promises us He will be with us in the hard times. *Isaiah 43:1-3 says, "Fear not, for I have redeemed you; I have summoned you by name; you are mine. When you pass through the waters, I will be with you, when you pass through the fire you will not be burned; the flames will not set you ablaze, for I am the Lord your God the Holy One of Israel, your Savior. . . "*

Or how about. . . *"God is my protection and my strength, and ever present help in trouble." Psalms 46:1.* (Aren't you glad you just learned the Bible is true!*)*

God is there! Ask any Christian who has gone through trials and tragedy, they will tell you they saw God move in unbelievable ways! In fact, I will. . .

In 1979, our son Jared, was born missing part of his heart – the aortic arch. That is the vessel that carries oxygenated blood out to the rest of the body. Because he was born without that tiny vessel, his organs weren't getting oxygenated blood and he was dying. Jared was rushed to a hospital in San Francisco when he was less than one day old. The surgeon, Dr. Robert Szarnicki, said he was going to "try something" to save our baby. To make a long story short, his "experiment" worked, and Jared became the first child on record to survive the surgery.

Jared was only in the hospital two weeks. Before we were able to take him home, his pediatric cardiologist, Dr. Robert Popper, described to us the procedure and told us what signs of distress to look for in Jared. They really didn't know what to expect because they had never had a survivor before Jared.

I'll never forget Dr. Popper's words. He said, "I can give you a hundred reasons why Jared should have died, I can't give you one why he lived." Needless to say, we told him – Jesus!

Now, how did I see God work in the midst of this, you ask? When I had Jared my doctor was on vacation. The doctor that filled in for him called the special team of doctors out of San Francisco. I found out later, my doctor would have called a team from Sacramento – Dr. Szarnicki's "experiment" would have never happened.

Dr. Szarnicki later shared he had gone to bed early that night, which was not his usual routine, so when he received the call to come to the hospital in the middle of the night, he was completely rested. Dr. Szarnicki also told us, "He had never had a surgery go so well."

There were many times I could feel Jesus right next to me. It defies description. Since this traumatic event, we have been able to share Jesus with so many people, many of whom have seen for the first time, Jesus is real, alive, and loves them.

God took that painful experience and turned it into something positive. If you trust Him and give your sorrows and pain to Him, He'll do the same for you as well.

- **"There are a bunch of hypocrites in church!"**

You are absolutely right – unfortunately. And there are a bunch of hypocrites outside churches as well, but don't blame God - He's not thrilled about it either! For some strange reason, God chose people to work through, and people are not perfect – never will be perfect – this side of heaven.

Remember, just 'cause you're in a garage – that doesn't make you a Chevy. Just 'cause you're in church – doesn't make you a Christian. God also says in the Bible *"Then I will tell them plainly, 'I never knew you. Away from me, you evildoers!'" Matthew 7:23*

If that's not bad enough, how about this?

"I know your deeds, that you are neither hot nor cold. I wish you were either one or the other! So, because you are lukewarm, neither hot nor cold, I am going to spit you out of my mouth." Revelation 3:15-16

That's super vomit, baby! How awful would that be to stand before God and have Him say to you... "I never knew you... away you evil person." Hypocrites and pretend Christians will pay a huge price. We can fool others, but we can't fool God. You see, God looks at the heart - not the pretty, or not-so-pretty packaging on the outside.

Hopefully, if you look deeper into the church you will find some "real" Christians – people who love others and give their lives and resources to help them.

- **"I'm not good enough for God. He wouldn't want me."**

If that were the case, *no one* would ever please God! Certainly, I am included. There is *not* a commandment I have not broken.

Let's look at some of the people in the Bible. They were *not* stained-glass saints. . . far from it!

Moses was a murderer.

Noah - what was the first thing he did when he hit dry ground? . . . He got drunk.

Abraham was a liar - but known as "a friend of God"

Jonah tried to run from God

Gideon was a coward

David was a murderer and adulterer - yet known as "a man after God's own heart."

How about some of Jesus' disciples:

Peter - was a "foot-in-the-mouth" kind of guy.

Matthew was a corrupt tax collector.

James and John were "hot heads."

And of course Paul – He pursued Christians and had them arrested, even executed – and he wrote most of the New Testament!

The people of the Old Testament had to do "something" to ask God for forgiveness – like sacrifice an animal – and then God forgave them.

New Testament people – once they met Jesus face to face, and accepted Him as God, they were not only forgiven, but their lives were changed forever.

The truth is – *you cannot do anything to clean yourself up for God*. God says to just come to Him and He'll take care of it. If we could clean ourselves up. . . Jesus would not have had to go to the cross! He paid that price for us - for which I know I'm thankful.

The people in the Bible were just like you and me. . . idiots a lot of the time! But God took their lives and made them spectacular!

- **"Do all roads lead to heaven?"**

If you read *any* of the first part of this book, and have come to the realization that the Bible is true - then the answer has to be a resounding NO! Jesus was a historical figure, written about in many sources other than the Bible. He did incredible miracles, again, all well documented. People were willing to allow themselves to be tortured to death because they swore to the fact they saw Jesus after his resurrection from the dead, and He is God. If all religions lead to heaven – why did Jesus do it? Why did he allow himself to be stripped, beaten beyond recognition, spat upon, humiliated, and finally hung on a cross like a common criminal to die a horrible, painful death?

Sorry guys. . . . just being a good person, feeding the poor, helping the sick, going on mission trips, eating all your broccoli, even helping old ladies across the street. . . . while they are all good things to do – your good "works" will not lead you to heaven. ONLY belief in Jesus Christ will do that. The Bible - which you now know to be true, says:

"If you declare with your mouth, "Jesus is Lord," and believe in your heart that God raised him from the dead, you will be saved.." Romans 10:9

- **"Many people say they don't believe the Bible"**

The truth is. . . usually, they have *never* even picked one up! They certainly have not gone to a Bible study to find out the true meaning. They only know what they've heard from others, possibly family members or friends. I beg you, check it out for yourself. Don't let the "nuts" on TV or radio who say dumb things like, "The world will end on May 21st at 6:00 p.m.," make you think all Christianity is wrong. (On that note, the Bible says clearly that NO ONE will know the time or day of Jesus' return.) *"But about that day or hour no one knows, not even the angels in heaven, nor the Son, but only the Father. Mark 13:32*

We've determined the Bible is true, and it clearly says you must believe in Jesus to have eternal life with Him.

"For God so loved the world He gave His one and only son, that whoever believes in Him shall not perish but have eternal life." John 3:16

THIS IS THE MOST IMPORTANT DECISION YOU WILL EVER MAKE. Will you choose to believe in Jesus? If you want to give your life to Christ, it's very simple. Just pray the "Sinner's Prayer," (yes, we are *all* sinners).

"Dear Lord, Please forgive my sins. I want You to live in my heart. I give my life to You. Amen."

That's all it takes. Jesus never intended it to be difficult for He wants *everyone* to be saved. But those few sentences will change your life forever, not just a week, a day or a few years. . . . *forever!*

If you accepted Jesus, please let someone know. Heck, please let me know! (cecile.kaiser@yahoo.com or heavenfun.com) Then, get into a "Bible-believing" church. *One that believes* **Jesus is God**, *not just* **a** *god, and not just a good teacher or a prophet*. You see, the threshold to heaven is - do you believe Jesus IS God and do you accept Him as your Savior?

"Jesus answered, I am the way and the truth and the life. No one comes to the Father except through me." John 14:6

Next, it is important to learn about the Bible and this wonderful God, Jesus. . . . who loved you so much, He gave His life for you.

SIXTEEN

"Verses You Can Rely On"

Now that you know this Bible is true. Here are some of my favorite verses.

GOD'S PROMISES

- John 10:28-29 "I give them eternal life, and they shall never perish; no one can snatch them out of my hand."
- Psalm 139: 17 "How precious to me are your thoughts, God! How vast is the sum of them!"

- Joshua 1:5b, Hebrews 13:5 & Deuteronomy 31:6 "I will never leave you or forsake you."

STRENGTH & WORRY

- Psalms 46:1" God is my protection and my strength, an ever present help in trouble."
- Isaiah 41:29 "He gives strength to the weary and increases the power of the weak."
- Matthew 11:28 "Come to me all who are weary and burdened and I will give you strength."
- Isaiah 43:1 "Fear not, for I have redeemed you; I have summoned you by name; you are mine. When you pass through the waters I will be with you.."
- Zephaniah 3:17 "The Lord your God is with you, he is mighty to save. He will take great delight in you, he will quiet you with his love, he will rejoice over you with singing."

FEAR

- Isaiah 41:13 "For I am the Lord your God, who takes hold of your right hand. Do not fear, I will help you."
- 1 Peter 5:14 "Cast all your cares on him for he cares for you
- Psalms 62:6 "He alone is my rock and my salvation; he is my fortress, I will not be shaken."

Don't miss Cecile's comedy devotional...

BEE OF GOOD CHEER
"A devotional for everyone who loves to laugh"

Chapter 1

"Gift? What Gift?"

"I look like my brother in this shirt!" I screamed at my mother in despair. I longed to look grown up, like Marilyn Monroe or Annette Funicello, or even some of my own friends. That's what prompted the actions that caused one the most embarrassing moments of my life. Let's face it, at 12 years old I truly believe the brain is not totally developed, ah... no pun intended. That wasn't the part I wanted developed anyway.

It was a hot summer day and I was anxious to wear my new bathing suit and go check out the "studs" at a neighborhood pool. Sure enough, they were there. Standing in the girl's bathroom, I looked at myself in the mirror, much to my frustration the new suit did not "enhance" anything. I reached into a stall and grabbed a handful of toilet paper and did my own enhancing. Wow, looked pretty good. If a little's pretty good, how about a bunch! I'll turn their heads now!

As I strutted around the pool, I noticed several guys eyeing me. You know, cat calls, whistles, loud obnoxious noises that must be a gene-thing or some ancient ritual that automatically ignites in boys around the age of 13. It was great. I lounged around on a towel. Sure enough, a couple of the "tribal members" came my way, pushing and shoving each other, even tossed a dead dragonfly at me, knowing I'd scream. Oh. . . they were interested. They sat down and we giggled awhile. Before long, my new friends thought it would be fun to throw me into the pool. In case this is a surprise to you, toilet paper does not do well in water. My new figure came out in every direction. And. . . I'm sure the boys, now men, will laugh about this incident until the day they die. I'm just *thrilled* I could bring joy to *their* lives. . . .

Ever long to be something you're not? Why is he or she so much better looking, more successful, have that terrific home or car, or whatever. . . . Or, if I could just be better, I'd do great things for God. Or. . .if I could just play the piano, I'd do great things for God. . . or if. . . and it goes

"Gift? What Gift?"

on and on. God does not ask that of us. He puts into your hand exactly what you need and helps you with the rest. God has a great sense of humor; look at some of the famous biblical leaders: Moses – the stutterer. God said, "What's in your hand?" Moses had a staff which he used to part the Red Sea. David – the "forgotten" son, had a sling and God said, "Let's go get Goliath." Peter and John – uneducated – had fishing nets and God made them "fishers of men." God does not ask us to be perfect human beings – just willing. Believe it or not, God made you just the way He wanted you. You need no enhancing (avoid toilet paper at any cost!). Whatever dream He has given you, whatever talent He has gifted you, that's your ministry. If it seems impossible – then it's from God – 'cause if you can do it by yourself – you wouldn't need God.

What's in your hand? What's on your heart? Give it to Jesus and He will use you through your gift.

"Dedicate to the Lord whatever you do, and your plans will succeed."

Proverbs 16:3.

ENDNOTES

· · ·

1. "Don't Check Your Brains at the Door," Word Publishing, Video series by Josh McDowell

2. "Don't Check Your Brains at the Door," Word Publishing, Video series by Josh McDowell

3. Stroble, Lee - *"A Case for Christ"* Zondervan Publishing - pg 78-80

4. Stroble, Lee *"Case for Christ,"* Zondervan Publishing, page 87

5. Stroble, Lee *"Case for Christ,"* Zondervan Publishing, page 87.

6. "Don't Check Your Brains at the Door," Word Publishing, Video series by Josh McDowell

7. "Don't Check Your Brains at the Door," Word Publishing, Video series by Josh McDowell

8. "Don't Check Your Brains at the Door," Word Publishing, Video series by Josh McDowell

9. "Don't Check Your Brains at the Door," Word Publishing, Video series by Josh McDowell

10. "Don't Check Your Brains at the Door," Word Publishing, Video series by Josh McDowell

11. "Don't Check Your Brains at the Door," Word Publishing, Video series by Josh McDowell

12. ALL of this information comes from "Don't Check Your Brains at the Door," Word Publishing, Video series by Josh McDowell.

13. http://www.reasons.org/fulfilled-prophecy-evidence-reliability-bible. Article by Dr. Hugh Ross, dated 8/22/2003

14. Article through joncourson.com, "A Physician Looks at Crucifixion" by Dr. Truman Davis.

15. http://www.reasons.org/articles/articles/fulfilled-prophecy-evidence-for-the-reliability-of-the-bible

16. http://bible.org/seriespage/bible-holy-canon-scripture

17. http://bible.org/seriespage/bible-holy-canon-scripture

18. "The New Evidence That Demands A Verdict," Josh McDowell, Nelson Publishing, 1999.

19. http://www.gotquestions.org/canon-Bible.html

20. "One Minute Answers to Skeptics," Campbell, Charlie H., Harvest House Publishers, Eugene Oregon, Copyright 2010, page 23-24.

21. http://www.gotquestions.org/canon-Bible.html

22. "One Minute Answers to Skeptics," Campbell, Charlie H., Harvest House Publishers, Eugene Oregon, Copyright 2010, page 21.

23. http://www.gotquestions.org/canon-Bible.html

24. Partially taken from "The Complete Bible Answer Book," 2004, by Hank Hanegraaff, Pg. 145-146.

25. "It Couldn't Just Happen," Pgs 127-131, by Lawrence O. Richards, 2011 Tommy Nelson Publishing

26. Partially taken from "The Complete Bible Answer Book," 2004, by Hank Hanegraaff, Pg. 170-171.

www.ingramcontent.com/pod-product-compliance
Ingram Content Group UK Ltd.
Pitfield, Milton Keynes, MK11 3LW, UK
UKHW041954230426
12048UKWH00008B/338